posh®

Coloring BOOK

· ·

VINTAGE DESIGNS
FOR FUN & RELAXATION

· ·

Andrews McMeel
Publishing®

Kansas City · Sydney · London

POSH® COLORING BOOK
Vintage Designs for Fun & Relaxation

Andrews McMeel Publishing, LLC
an Andrews McMeel Universal company
1130 Walnut Street, Kansas City, Missouri 64106

www.andrewsmcmeel.com

15 16 17 18 19 MLY 10 9 8 7

ISBN: 978-1-4494-5876-8

www.shutterstock.com
With thanks to Hannah Davies for her original artworks

ATTENTION: SCHOOLS AND BUSINESSES
Andrews McMeel books are available at quantity discounts with bulk purchase for educational, business, or sales promotional use. For information, please e-mail the Andrews McMeel Publishing Special Sales Department: specialsales@amuniversal.com.

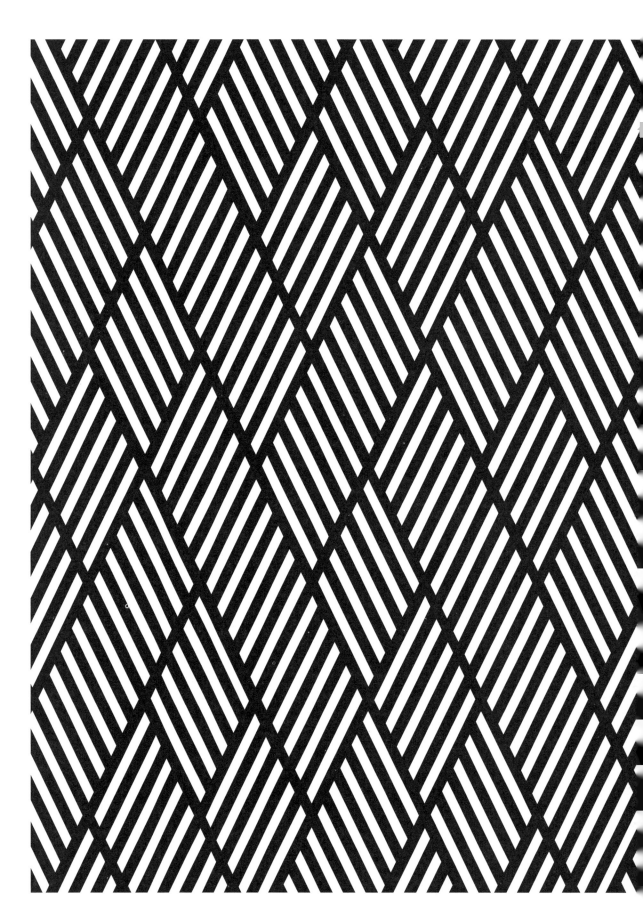

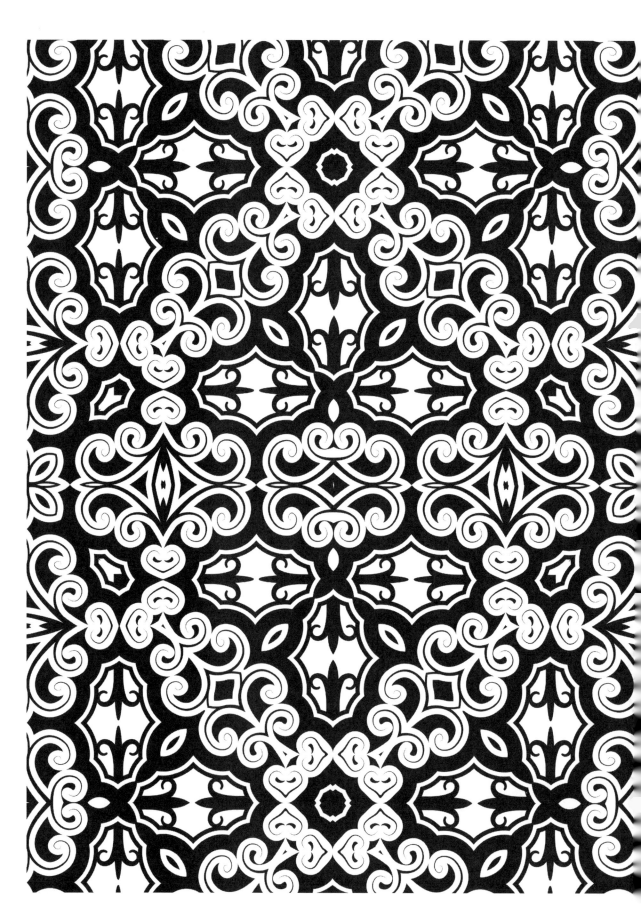